Desiderata for the Business Owner

∴

Adapted by Stephen Jones from
Max Ehrmann's original poem

Introduction

I grew up as a forces kid, which meant moving a lot. My Father was a fighter pilot in the R.A.F. I was born in Germany, and moved every two and a half to three years.

From Germany to the UK, to Scotland, Germany again, France, UK, and then to Cornwall when he retired.

All that time, there was one strange constant - a copy of Max Ehrmann's poem Desiderata hung on the loo door. That poem followed us around Europe like one of those puppies from a Disney movie...

I used to read it pretty much every day, and I like to think that it had arguably the biggest impact on how, and why, I live my life the way I have. I often think back on my career, and wonder just how much the original poem influenced my thinking.

Did it encourage me to start my own business as a kid? Probably, and I still am learning the lessons it taught me today.
From having a venture capital company to selling pizzas, it made no difference, I knew that I would always respect the opinion of others.

I have been equally at home in the corporate board room, working from home, and working in a cafe in a third world country.

I realised that where you are in life doesn't diminish your ability, intelligence, or authority.

My career has taken me from selling cleaning services as a child, through corporate sales, and then into self employment again.

Initially, as a backpacker in Oz, I worked with companies as a "mole" in their sales team. I was just a new hire here to learn the ropes. Then providing the CEO with a full report on the sales team by the end of week 1.

From there I moved to the US to tour around on a motorcycle for a year, before getting into telephone Investment sales (Think Wolf of Wall Street, without the drugs, hookers, dwarves, and theft issues).

I then established my own Venture Capital Firm without really knowing what Venture Capital was.

After losing it all, I started back up as a Business and Capital Advisor. I lost it all a second time for very different reasons and ended up making pizzas on the side of a volcano in Chile.

During that time I only avoided becoming homeless because a friend let me stay in his Cabin. I'm now back in the UK with a US based hedge fund, a small business advisory firm, and a new CIC designed to help children with mental health issues in sport.

It has been a fun ride, with most of my guiding principles throughout being the words of the Poem.

The one hanging on the back of a toilet door...

I often wonder what my life would have been if they had just put up a picture!

I think everyone can gain something from reading the original. However, I had always wanted to make it relevant for Small Business Owners and how they operate on a day to day basis.

I was hoping it would end up being a masterpiece, several chapters long, but in the end, simple is better. So here is my take on Desiderata for the Small Business Owner!

I would like to thank the following people:

- My parents - for hanging the thing up in the first place
- Jane Propert - for encouraging me to write this
- Nikkie Jay - for her copy writing 'extraordinaire"

- Brad Burton, 'Uncle' Croz Crossley, and Conor Stanage for letting me refer to them, and for the lessons they provided!

Stephen Jones
The Business Disruptor TM

Desiderata

GO PLACIDLY amid the noise and the haste, and remember what peace there may be in silence.
As far as possible, without surrender, be on good terms with all persons.
Speak your truth quietly and clearly; and listen to others, even to the dull and the ignorant; they too have their story.
Avoid loud and aggressive persons; they are vexatious to the spirit.
If you compare yourself with others, you may become vain or bitter, for always there will be greater and lesser persons than yourself.
Enjoy your achievements as well as your plans.
Keep interested in your own career, however humble; it is a real possession in the changing fortunes of time.
Exercise caution in your business affairs, for the world is full of trickery.
But let this not blind you to what virtue there is; many persons strive for high ideals, and everywhere life is full of heroism.
Be yourself. Especially do not feign affection.
Neither be cynical about love; for in the face of all aridity and disenchantment, it is as perennial as the grass.
Take kindly the counsel of the years, gracefully surrendering the things of youth.

Nurture strength of spirit to shield you in sudden misfortune.
But do not distress yourself with dark imaginings.
Many fears are born of fatigue and loneliness. Beyond a wholesome discipline, be gentle with yourself.
You are a child of the universe no less than the trees and the stars; you have a right to be here. And whether or not it is clear to you, no doubt the universe is unfolding as it should.
Therefore be at peace with God, whatever you conceive Him to be.
And whatever your labours and aspirations, in the noisy confusion of life, keep peace in your soul.
With all its sham, drudgery and broken dreams, it is still a beautiful world.
Be cheerful.
Strive to be happy.

By Max Ehrmann © 1927 - Original text

Go placidly amid the noise and haste, and remember what peace there may be in silence

Noise and haste…
Never in the history of human existence has the pace become so frantic.

My Great Grandfather was born in the late 1800's before Max Ehrmann had written the original poem. He used to talk to me about how "crowded" the world had become since he was a lad.

How they used to have people lighting the gas lamps in the street, horses and carts were replaced by noisy machines, and I got that.

But information was still something that you had to seek out.

Consumption was an illness, not an economic term.

There was nothing being broadcast except "the Wireless", let alone phones that can be used to con, scam, or bully you.

We are truly living noisy times, social media is ruining peoples ability to interact face to face, it is creating an environment of hatred, envy, and jealousy.
Then there are tools such as Alexa are making people ruder and more demanding.

Peace in Silence...

In amongst all of this noise, and fake businesses, magic diet pills, and overnight solutions for success, it is harder than ever to stand out from the crowd without making noise.
To quote my Great Grandfather (Not his words) "Walk softly, but carry a big stick!".
There are genuine people out there, humble people who walk calmly through the maelstrom, making their voice heard without resorting to yelling from the roof tops.
For over 7,000 years people have been using meditation as a way to calm their inner self.
There is a genuine peace to be found in just sitting quietly and reflecting on things, which is basically what meditation is.

In Practice...

The "scammiest" of the scams shout loudly from the highest rooftop about how good they are because they have to.

They have to have the glitziest marketing, the best videos and the biggest promises.

But here is the thing, they don't have to produce anything; not in the end.

Those who are honest tend to walk quietly and humbly.

So when you are in a networking event, look at the guy who wants a 1-2-1 before knowing who you are, he wants to go on about how good he is at (Insert business here) and how everyone buys from him. Of course they don't, these are just "Leads" he has mentally converted into clients.

He is not interested in you, what you do, or even if you need his product. You are simply there to be sold "AT". Talk with pride about what you do, but do not force it onto people.
Do not assume everyone you meet is a potential client or lead. They may be, but if you are not interested in them, they will have none in you.

Remember, people buy people, so walk quietly and back up your actions with underselling, over delivering, and excellent customer service.

As far as possible without surrender, be on good terms with all persons

Without Surrender...

I am assuming you are a good person at heart, otherwise you would probably have stopped reading this by now. (If you are not, and you haven't; feel free to do so!)

I also assume you have a certain morality. A networking friend of mine Conor Stanage makes and sells amazing watches, he also sources rare and hard to find pieces for clients.

However, he draws the line at dealing in old Nazi watches.

Occasionally he will be asked to find one, he turns it down, and the person gets agitated.

Conor is not prepared to trade his beliefs for business!

In the same way, one should not feel the need to be on good terms with someone who stands for everything you oppose.

When you are out and about networking, working with clients, prospects and so on, you will inevitably meet people who are difficult at best!

◆◆◆

Be on good terms with all persons…

This part of the poem for me covers "Burning Bridges", I have only ever burned 2 bridges… Both are ex wives!

I have a vivid recollection of helping a guy out who was in a networking group I ran I Kuwait.
He was an older guy and no one really knew what he did. I spent two half days at his house, helping him define what he did and how to offer it to people.

A week later, I walked into the networking meeting, he couldn't see me, but was happily telling everyone what an £$@% I was…..?????!!!!!
I could have lost it, kicked him out of the group etc. Instead I sat down and asked him to explain to me what I had done wrong in his eyes to warrant such comments.

His ethos didn't offend me, he wasn't a racist or an extremist religious person. I didn't have to go the extra mile, but I firmly believe in finding the best in people and situations.

Imagine how much my credibility increased when instead of throwing him out of the group I worked to resolve the issue.

Acting like a mature, sensible grown up pays dividends in areas we can't even begin to imagine.

Practical terms...

If you find yourself being trolled on social media or talked about behind your back in networking groups, remember that the person doing it to you is more than likely doing it to others.

It is more of a reflection on them, than yourselves. If you find yourself being drawn in by the statements and questions of others such as,
"How can you let them get away with saying XXX about you", simply smile.
Then say something disarming like, "I'm not sure what would cause them to say anything like that about me, I am sure they have their reasons, even if it's based on a misunderstanding", and then move the conversation on.

If it is an issue that won't go away, or has the ability to impact on your business, speak to whoever is in charge of the networking group and ask if they can "mediate" a conversation between the two of you.

Speak your truth quietly and clearly; and listen to others, even the dull and the ignorant; they too have their story

Speak your truth quietly and clearly… Tying in with "Go Placidly", you don't need to shout about your product from the highest rooftop, nor push it into everyone's face.

By talking about what you do openly, honestly and calmly, you will reach the ears of those who need what you have to sell.

Imagine for a moment a young person on limited income desires a new BMW.
He knows he can't afford it, but he wants it.
Instead he buys a second hand old rust bucket, because it is all that he can afford at that moment.

Would BMW run around trying to persuade him to buy from them?

Would they drop their price?

Of course not.

Their quality, integrity, and reputation stand.

They will not drop the price to suit one individual.

Yet small business owners tend to do it weekly. If not daily!

People aspire to be able to afford the car of their dreams. It doesn't have to be "Sold", in fact the more they wait, the greater the desire becomes.
So by sticking to your pricing and being able to justify why it is where it is and why you will not compromise on quality gives you that same integrity and authority.

Listen to others...

Having an open mind is essential in life!

"If you are the smartest person in the room, you are in the wrong room"...

Confucius was spot on.

However, this does not mean you are unable to learn from those who may appear dull, or ignorant.

There are many people I have worked with who were virtually idiot savants, they struggled to communicate, especially at a networking event.

Yet once you peeled back the "dull" exterior I usually found a genius who was unable to communicate well.

Likewise, I have hired people as cold callers who clearly had issues from an educational point. Nonetheless, they have often fed me some amazing lines to use, because they are approaching life from a very different perspective.

They see things differently, and not from the same angle as those you surround yourself with daily.

It is one of the things I love most about having lived and worked in so many countries; you meet people that are often classed as 'Poor', 'ignorant', or even 'Dumb', yet by having an open mind, you can glean so much from their point of view and learn a lot.

If you listen to others around you, you will recognise the clues that tell you who needs what you have.

Ask open ended questions and actually listen to the replies. If you are talking to dull and/or ignorant people, take it as an opportunity to see what you can learn from people who see life differently to you.

Practical terms...

Particularly with regard to networking, or interacting with others, try to take the time to listen to everyone in the room.
Do not be dismissive of the person who seems to stutter, falter or fail to explain clearly what it is they do.

As an active listener, you can actually help these people refine how they talk about what they do, and raise them up. Don't miss an opportunity to help, it shows you in a good light and makes you feel better about yourself.
Talk about you, your services or products humbly and explain it in simple terms so your prospective clients can understand.

Create a scenario where they feel comfortable approaching you to buy.

Avoid loud and aggressive persons, they are vexations to the spirit

Loud & aggressive persons...
We all know them. It usually starts with the bully at school, or the know-it-all who actually knows very little, and understands less.

Remember: "Dumb isn't loud because it is right. It is loud because it is dumb"!
Having spent time talking about being humble, walking softly, talking quietly about who you are and what you do, it is time for the "Why", why do we act like that?

What is the alternative?
People who fit into this category are not to be confused with those who are larger than life or the life and soul of the party.

It refers to the brash, obnoxious type, those who speak inappropriately, uses crass, racist, or sexist remarks, and ignores the feelings of those around them.

It can also be the type who has to crush your hand when they shake, or who slaps you on the back hard enough to break it.

All of these people have something to prove, and usually are the last to admit, or recognise it.

You can, (and bitter experience has taught me this), spend a lot of time trying to lift someone up like this, only to find out they are quite happy where they are and have no interest in changing.

Unless you make your money as a psychologist, or similar, avoid the headache!

Vexations to the Spirit...
In the long run, people who don't want to change drain you, spiritually and mentally.

The best advice is ignore them where possible. They will only put you in a state of annoyance, frustration, or worry.

These negative vibrations ripple out in 'Your pond' to create negativity in others around you.

It's why, when you are having a bad day, everything goes wrong.

Negativity breeds negativity. Ignore them, walk away, allow them to paint you in whatever language they choose to others.

The people that count will recognise them for what they are.

In practical terms…

Have you ever been at an event where a loud and aggressive personality assaults your senses? It is tiring, frustrating, and annoying.

These people are incapable of listening, or changing. They will bring no benefit to your organisation either as an employee or as a client. Avoid them!

Learn to recognise them quickly, be pleasant, swap cards, and move on. If there are two at an event and one is talking to you, use the line "Hey XX, have you met YY? I think you two have a lot to discuss" and then leave them to it.

If you compare yourself with others, you may become vain and bitter; for always there will be greater and lesser persons than yourself

Compare yourself with others...
"I'm not as successful as my competitors."; "XYZ firm is not getting as many clients as us."

Two things I hate to hear when talking with a new client.

I often quote this poem to them when they say it.

It demonstrates that their focus in business is on what the competitors are doing, not on what they are doing, which is invariably why they are doing badly.

Too much time spent looking at the wrong markers and playing catch-up is exhausting.

My favourite quote on this comes from the old apple launches, where the back rows were full of competitor salespeople and engineers: 'Innovate, create, do not follow.' Not one apple employee attended a Microsoft presentation!

It is also worth reading The Infinite game by Simon Sinek on this!!

You may become vain and bitter...

Inevitably, if you find yourself comparing you and your achievements to others, you will spiral down into bitterness.
If you see yourself as better than other, vanity will take over and you become more focussed on the image of success, rather than actual success.

Greater and lesser persons...

At no point in human history has this been more important than now, with social media showing the 'perfect life', 'perfect business', 'laptop lifestyle' when the reality is far from it.
Suicides are at an all time high, as is depression and divorces. I am convinced that this is a direct result of people comparing themselves to people around them who appear to have a perfect life.

I try to explain to my children that these images are false, or snapshots. There are lots of photos online of a friend of mine smiling and happy; yet he took his own life.
There are many people who will achieve more than you, and many others who achieve less.
Some of the former will not be as happy as you, and some of the latter will be happier. That is just perspective.

In practical terms...

Remember that as you look through social media you are only seeing a snapshot of their life.

When you meet people at networking events they are 'On Show' and in selling mode, not everything is as it appears.
I used to attend an event with a guy who talked like he owned a mansion, luxury cars and had the perfect lifestyle.
He was always impeccably dressed, yet it turned out he lived in a studio flat above a pound shop in one of the dodgiest areas of town and was barely making enough to get by.

It was all an image, a facade.

Be yourself, speak your truth and understand that there will always be someone better off and someone worse off than you. Be happy in your now!
Croz Crossley took the teachings from the science of getting rich, he learnt them, and implemented them, he now teaches them to others.

The line he uses that made me think of him for this section is 'Holiday Mind'.

Holiday mind is where when you have booked a holiday, you think about it in terms of relaxing on the beach or skiing down your favourite slopes, or other positive thoughts based on your preferred type of holiday.

You don't sit there thinking about the possible delayed flights, or the potential to break a limb, or getting sick.

In essence, you focus on the good things to come and therefore create positive vibes.

Enjoy your achievements as well as your plans.

Enjoy your Achievements...

With so much negativity around us and so many doubters, you have to celebrate the every win, even if you consider it small.

Got a new lead from a new networking group? Fantastic, celebrate!

These little wins add up, they create positivity, and positivity breeds positivity.

If in doubt, try an experiment: Walk into your office, team, pub, or home in a great mood, no matter how you are feeling and see how the day/evening turns out.

Then do it again; but next time in a bad mood, and compare the results.

Your plans...

This is the bit that fits in with Croz's message:

Enjoy your plans.

If you are setting up a new business, hiring someone new, starting an exercise regime, whatever the plan is, focus on the positives:

What will life look like, feel like, and be like when it is successful?

Then, when you find yourself doubting things - which you will..... go back to those positive thoughts.

Obviously consider the issues, and mitigate against them, but think and draw on the positives.

In practical terms...

When we make a plan of action for your business, a new marketing approach, a new product or approaching a new client, we often do it with a sense of foreboding.

A friend who had a drilling company in Texas used to call it 'Eeyore Syndrome'.

Always looking for the cloud attached to the silver lining.

Instead of imaging the worst, write down what the possible hurdles and downsides are, mitigate against them, and then run it through the decision tree.

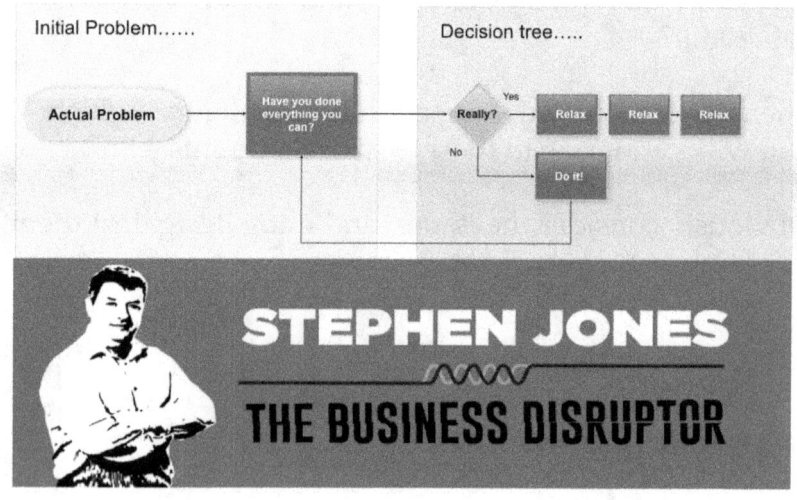

The Business disruptor systemising Croz's "Have I done everything I can" statement….

Keep interested in your own career, however humble; it is a real possession in the changing fortunes of time

Interest in your own career...

So many clients I work with have 'Lost their Mojo' and will tell me so; usually using the exact words "I have lost interest in what I do"!

The spark has gone.

Unfortunately during the day to day hustle and bustle, the slog and the grind, we lose sight of what we are doing and why.
A lot of my work involved finding that spark, and re-igniting it.

We need to keep hold of the passion for doing what we do and rekindle it if we have lost it.

A real possession...

Another way to look at this is this; When growing up, I used to buy and sell stuff and work in kitchens. If all else were to fail, I could fall back on either and make enough money to survive and rebuild (I know because I had no choice but to do this in Chile).

Having a 'Back-stop' means that no matter how daunting the road ahead, if the worst came to the worst and the fortunes changed against you, you could fall back to that position.

Practical terms...
Once you know what your 'Back-stop' is, you can relax a lot more in the decisions you are taking in your business. If the passion has faded, then just as you should with a relationship, rediscover that original spark, the thing that fired you up when you first started.

If you have not lost it, or if you have got it back after losing it then nurture the passion, and embrace what you do with all the vigour you had at the start.

Exercise caution in your business affairs; for the world is full of trickery.

Caution in your business affairs...

I think most of us know how easy it is to be conned, or taken for a ride and not just from the out and out scammers.
I have a young lad I am helping for free, he doesn't have a company yet, but he will do, and I know we will develop business together in the future.

He was in front of some smart franchised 'Business Coach' who was urging him to buy a monthly coaching plan.

This guy doesn't even have a company.

Incorrigible!

The world is full of trickery...

Trickery

From the slick marketing guys who bore you with 'Success story' marketing campaigns telling you how to get thousands of people into your funnel. When you could only sell to one or two people a week and only deliver to one or two; To the guys telling you that you can sell like they can by paying hundreds to attend their event, only to be told to pay thousands to buy into their VIP circle and so on.

Let us not even delve into the world of over sellers who under deliver.

1. If it sounds too good to be true - IT IS!
2. If you don't need hundreds of new clients, don't buy anything that aims to deliver it.
3. If someone is promising you everything you need by the date you need it; question it!

Practical terms...

How often do we see a posting on social media along the lines of "Has anyone used XXX company for YYY service?" "We did and they charged ZZZ, promising to do EVERYTHING we asked for, by the date we wanted it, and delivered nothing/rubbish/etc..."

This is over-selling, and under delivering which guaranteed to lose you clients.

In business sales I strive to teach my students that underselling and over delivering is the way to go, it creates incredibly happy clients that will shout about you to anyone who listens.

So we need to turn this on its head when we are buying.

There is a reason why corporates ask for three detailed quotes, although that system is being abused.

The idea was always to compare the service/product as a like for like and then compare pricing based on the criteria selected.

We need to employ those ideals when buying from "Specialists" we encounter.

I worry more when someone says, "Yes I can" than when they say, "Actually, I am not sure if I can do that" or, "do that by that time" because it usually infers they are saying anything to get the work and there is usually a reason why they need the work so badly.

Ask questions, question the reply, and the motives. Shop around, and ask for reviews BEFORE you buy.

But let this not blind you to what virtue there is in the world. Many people strive for high ideals and everywhere life is full of heroism

Blind you to what virtue...

Despite all of the above, you should not let this cautionary tale deter you from opening up new opportunities, the world would truly be a dull place if we hid in our own corners and didn't reach out once in a while.

Life is full of heroism...

Many people are genuine, and many of the 'falling outs' that we witness could have been averted much earlier through discussion, and clarification.

It is why I keep pushing the idea of "Underselling and over-delivering" as an ethos.

I want to ensure that during the sales process you avoid what is referred to as mutual mystification.

Mutual mystification is the confusion that arises by assuming the other party knows exactly what you are saying, without questioning it properly.
There are true heroes in the world and some you will encounter every day.

In business there are those who are honest, forthright, and trying to achieve the best for their clients with the solution they offer.

Seek them out, find them, connect with them!

Practical terms...

Success breeds success:

Do not flounder around looking for suppliers, get out and network.

If someone approaches you, find out about them, do your homework. Do others work with them? What was their experience? Are there any bad reviews online?

As with issues that may arise from a new decision or plan, mitigate the problems you may face when working with someone new!

Be yourself. Especially do not feign affection

Be yourself....

… Because everyone else is taken! (I love that quote)
But truly, a guy I follow and admire, Brad Burton, takes the 'Marmite' approach to its conclusion by showing you how the very reason one person hates you, is the same reason another likes you.
Never try to adapt to fit the expectations of others.

In sales, be yourself, know what type of client you prefer to work with and seek them out during your qualification stage.

If someone does not fit into your way of working, then they are not a prospective client, they are a prospective pain in the arse.

It took me a long time to come to terms with this. I still struggle!

Having been involved in sales all my life, I have been 'Mirroring', 'Emulating'. 'Fitting in' so much that when my first wife and I separated, I sat at home and realised I was crying over a box of chocolates.

Not because we had split up, but because all my life I had eaten whatever chocolate my mother or wife didn't want.

I had never actually opened a box a chocolate and chosen what I wanted.

I still struggle with the need to have people 'Like me', but as I get older it get easier!

Especially, do not feign affection....

This fits in nicely with the above statement.
If you met a prospect at their office, and it was clear that their entire ethos was in conflict with yours, would you want to work with them?
Would you fake similar interests just to get the sale?

I know people and industries that do, often, and they have huge attrition rates; buyer's remorse.

If you are sitting on the fence on this one, imagine walking into a prospects office, and seeing Nazi memorabilia everywhere, and a picture of Hitler on the wall.

Would you compromise now?

If this seems a bit far fetched, remember my friend Conor Stanage how often he gets asked to source Nazi watches for some VERY strange people.

Neither be cynical about love; for in the face of all aridity and disenchantment it is as perennial as the grass

Love may be a bit strong a term in the business world, but some people are going to 'get you', and some will champion you and your cause.

Don't readily dismiss this or feel embarrassed by it, embrace it and find your own heroes to champion.

You can also consider the fact that you should "Love what you do"… it amazes me how many people spend their life in a '9-5' job that they don't enjoy, looking forward to a retirement they can't afford….

The sagest advice I ever heard on the matter is "Find something you love to do, and get paid for it, and never work a day in your life"…. It is never quite THAT easy, but by working in your passion - the harder days will be more bearable!!

Take kindly the counsel of the years, gracefully surrendering the things of youth

The counsel of years...

The essence of this for me is learning from your mistakes and experiences.

I often hear the opening line of "If you could; where would you go back to in your life and take a different path?"

Having divorced twice, with a child from each that I am raising. Having lost my fortune twice, ended up stranded and all but homeless in Chile. Having sat on the wall of a harbour contemplating the unthinkable jump, there are many 'Diversion points' I could go back to and change.

However, that would then take away from who I am and who I have become.

Each experience, both good and bad shapes us.

How we handle the rejection, failure, and disappointment is how we become a stronger, better person.

But, we have to be able to sit back, and reflect on those decisions while trying our best to learn from them.

surrendering the things of youth...

I always struggled with this part of the poem. I have always been youthful in nature, still like to have fun, it was only when I really thought about it that it started to make sense.

I no longer play Rugby because I can't afford to take time out with broken bones.

I no longer leave clothes scattered around the house, because my kids need to learn to pick up after themselves.

I no longer head out for a party till all hours of the morning because I know that the next day I have 2 kids to take care of.

So while we do remain 'young at heart', we also gradually surrender the things of youth, replacing them with something better; Wisdom and experience!

Nurture strength of spirit to shield you in sudden misfortune

Life is hard, so is business. In the old days people talked about a 'Thick Skin' and how sticks and stones may break your bones.

Unfortunately today, society seems to have changed with verbal bullying, offensive hate speech, and derisory comments appearing to have far more impact on people than before.

I stand by the old ways, I believe in strengthening your mind as you would your body, to face any onslaught.

A strength of Spirit can be likened to a fighter's mind set. You know you are going to get knocked about, even down, but you don't quit.

Sometimes you get beaten, but that is the nature of both the game and life.

I shared a video a while back of a bison being pulled down by a pride of lions, it just lay there, as good as dead.

Then the lionesses started fighting, the males got involved, and they were all so busy that the bison just got up and walked away.

He didn't stay lying down!

Fight for yourself and abandon the "Victim mentality" where everything that is wrong in your life is someone else's fault.

But do not distress yourself with dark imaginings. ...

Back to Uncle Croz and his teaching around holiday mindset.

We tend to fear the unknown, and those early mornings, when all is dark and quiet, and we replay issues in our heads, thinking of all the things that can go wrong….

We have to empty that decision tree with each of the thoughts - Have I done everything I can? - If no - make a quick note of the things you can still do, if yes… dismiss it, and move on…

I also find thinking about the positive outcomes helps, so if you have a tough negotiation coming up with a client, imagine how it is going to feel when they accept your proposal, and you complete the work for them…

Instead of thinking about the worst case scenario and dragging yourself down, think more about the positives and the good that can come from the future event/action you are planning.

Of course things can go wrong, and inevitably do - especially with a difficult customer, all we can do as part of our planning is to consider them, note them, and then plan solutions to overcome them.

AS the old saying goes….

Hope for the best, but plan for the worst!

Many fears are born of fatigue and loneliness

Ever had it? That time you wake up at 3am, and everything is wrong with everything.

You can't sleep, tossing and turning, then eventually you fall into a fitful doze.

Later on standing in the shower, trying to rouse yourself, you cannot for the life of you remember what you were worried about?

No good decision comes from a position of stress and angst.

Military training is all about preparing people to make quick decisions under immense pressure, whilst taking away the ability to 'Decide' based on their own interpretations.

As an example: My Father was a fighter pilot, part of his career he spent flying Nuclear weapons strapped under his wings, ready to deploy if he was told to.

His ability to think under pressure was incredible, split second decisions flying at Mach whatever. But if told to fire, he was trained to do it.

No thinking about casualties, the effect on the civilians, just do the job he was trained for.

Fortunately, in our lives, we don't tend to carry that sort of pressure or responsibility. We can often act as though what we are doing IS life or death… and with none of the training that he received!

It is imperative that when trying to make a critical decision for your life, or businesses, you step back, calm down.

Assess the facts not the emotions, and move from a position of strength.

Beyond a wholesome discipline, be gentle with yourself

We can all beat ourselves up about a lost deal, a forgotten appointment, a sick day that was a bit 'weak'.
Whilst it is important to keep yourself accountable and disciplined, we are not all Shaolin Monks, we do not have to be hard on ourselves all the time.

I used to give a talk where I would start by asking who had their own business; then who could take a day off without it failing; or a week, a month, a year?

There would always be ONE with their had up at the end…!
But to the rest I would say:

"You are not business owners, but self employed, you have a job that you are tied to… and congratulations, you have the world's worst boss."

Why?

Because as you've had a great week you 'treat' yourself by knocking off early on Friday to celebrate.

Then what happens when you are having a bad week? You take off early on Friday to 'Regroup'.

We need a certain amount of discipline as business owners. Creating systems, processes, and targets means we can ensure we are on, and stay on track.

But we have to cut ourselves some slack from time to time, and not overcomplicate things!

You are a child of the universe, no less than the trees and the stars; you have a right to be here

Echoing back to the earlier part where we discussed strength of Spirit, many people seem to feel they don't belong, or that they are not as equal as others.
We are all born with the same potential. The experiences and circumstances of life will only define us if we allow them to.

At a recent 'Single Parent Information Program' people were talking about the effect that hearing their parents arguing constantly might have on the children's future.

My answer was not 'normal' when I pointed out that all these 'super-successful' people tend to have a bad experience in their past that motivated them to go onto better things.

Irrespective of who you are, where you were born, or how you were brought up, you have a right to life, and have just as much right to be here as anyone else.

I frequently Judge people around me by how they treat people 'below them' in station. How a businessman treats wait staff, janitors, cleaners etc reflects on them.

If you don't respect someone for who they are, you won't respect them for their job.

And whether or not it is clear to you, no doubt the universe is unfolding as it should

Ever notice how when you are having a bad day everything goes wrong?

Dropping your toast, it lands butter side down. You are running late, get out of the house, forget your phone, go back to find it, can't then realise its in the pocket you were looking in before. You get down the road, some idiot cuts you up, then you get stuck behind someone driving at 20mph below the speed limit.... And so it continues.

What is the difference between that, and a good day? The day you catch the toast, phew that was close. You realise your phone is in your pocket before traipsing back into the house. You let a guy out in front of you, and enjoy a great song as you relax on the way into work. It's the same day, the same person, just a different attitude.

It startles me how many people are willing to believe that your mood has NO effect on things, but not willing to admit that it could.

I don't believe in fate, but I do believe that if you decide what you want, make a plan on how you can get it and then work the plan, by some strange miracle, you will get it.

How many times have you been at a networking event knowing you needed to talk to someone who could help with XXX and then they just happen to be there and they want to talk to you?

We always used to use the adage 'The harder I work, the luckier I get', and I think this fits nicely here, negativity breeds negativity, and I started to suffer from this whilst living in Chile - no matter what I did, it went wrong... Everything......

I was blaming everyone but myself, and eventually, woke up to my mistake! I took a very low paid Job 1000km away from home, but it was a place I loved, and the job was basic maintenance and riding of motorcycles for a tour operator in Patagonia... (Nice work if you can get it) but it was the start of my "Stopping the downward spiral" and moving forward with a new plan, new approach, and it worked... 'Insert shocked face picture' (In house Joke with Croz!)

Therefore be at peace with God, whatever you conceive Him to be, and whatever your labours and aspirations, in the noisy confusion of life keep peace with your soul Be at peace with God

Whatever religion or belief system you follow.....

As Dave Allen used to say, "If you have a God, may that god go with you".

Being religious, or spiritual is not the sole domain of organised religion, or its followers.

I would rather deal with a person who did not believe in god, but who had their own moral code and stuck to it, than work with a religious person who eschewed the teachings of their religion.

You have to sleep at night, you have to justify your actions to yourself in those lonely 3am discussions when you can't sleep.

Have a moral compass, and follow it!

It never ceases to amaze me how many people still hand in money they find, and how many people live by the rules of society, when all around them people are doing pretty much whatever they want… That shows real moral fortitude, even more so if they are no religious, and living under the fear of eternal damnation!!

Many people you will come across in business will be the same, they would rather do the right thing, and lose a bit, rather than do the wrong thing and win… these are the people you want to work with on joint ventures, and strategic alliances!

With all its sham, drudgery, and broken dreams, it is still a beautiful world

If I look out of my window, I can see the same scene in two different ways:

I can see a dirty town centre with a group of youths hanging around, rubbish in the gutter, and cars parked illegally…

Or, I can see the person that just dropped their papers in the road and the car that stopped to help them. The kids enjoying the afternoon sun, the trees, and the pretty baskets of flowers business owners have bought to make the town look nice.

It is the same view, I acknowledge the sham and drudgery, I watch for threats, but I still stop to smell the flowers……

Be cheerful.

As with the above, being happy is not something that can be done later when you have the money/house/partner/car or other 'Must have thing', it is a choice.

Throughout my life I have suffered hardships and problems, yet I choose, for the main, to be happy.

Is it easy? Of course not - I mentioned the victim mentality earlier that I found myself in the grip of, it was not the only time I caught myself slipping, and that is OK, because once you notice it, you can fix it…

Having a cheerful disposition rubs off on those around you, and breeds a similar spirit in your entire life…

Strive to be happy

It isn't a magic formula:

"I think I'm happy so I am, and nothing bothers me."

You have to work at it, you have to enjoy those small wins, ignore the haters, or the loud and obnoxious people.

You have to walk away from the bad people in your life and be prepared to say, 'Enough', when you need to.

Striving to be happy is THE way to ensure you will be - as with being cheerful, it takes work, but when you find yourself in that sad place, it is worth noting what is making you sad, and analysing what you can do to fix that issue.

As with anything, once you have identified the issue, and created a plan to fix it, if you follow the plan, you WILL get results!

Conclusion...

These last two "lines" feed into my theory on mind-set and what I call the three mind sets of the average human:

Victim Mentality
Where everything that happens or happened to you is everyone else's fault, and you blame them for your problems.

Comfort Zone Mentality
AKA "I'm all right" mentality, where everything is 'Fine' or 'OK' and people are going through the motions of life

Winning Mentality
Where the person is driven and doesn't accept mediocrity. Is driven because of the things that happened to them. Accepts that it may be someone else's fault, but that how they react to it is their choice. Does not do 'Comfort Zones'.

But I am thinking this requires another mini-book!

In the meantime, you can listen to all the Guru's self help guys and others all you want. But unless you find the switch inside you and flip it yourself, you will not be the best version of you.
You have to turn on that desire to be successful, whatever that success may look like to you at this point in your life.

Remember, the way we measure success differs, and the goals we set in life are moveable and ever changing.

When I was a kid, I wanted to be Superman, my goals changed!!

Life is only here once, as far as we can prove, and all in all it isn't that long.

So why not enjoy it while you are here?

Thanks for reading this all the way through!!!

Regards,

Stephen Jones - The Business Disruptor

www.ingramcontent.com/pod-product-compliance
Lightning Source LLC
Chambersburg PA
CBHW070817220526
45466CB00002B/694